IN THESE HILLS

IN THESE HILLS

A Collection of Poems and Drawings
of Grand Portage, Minnesota

Poems by Joanne Hart
Drawings by Jayne Gagnon

Women's Times Publishing
Grand Marais, Minnesota

Poems were first published:
"First Cold," "Rules for Winter" in *Dacotah Territory;*
"Bear Grazing," "Where I Bathe" in *Women's Times;*
"Powwow" in *Milkweed Chronicle;*
"Twelve Miles to the School Bus" in *Great River Review.*

In These Hills. Copyright © 1982 Joanne Hart. Drawings © 1982 by Jayne Gagnon. Printed and bound in Canada. All rights reserved. No part of this book may be reproduced in any form or by any electronic or mechanical means including information storage and retrieval systems without permission in writing from the publisher, except by a reviewer, who may quote brief passages in a review. For information contact: Women's Times Publishing, P.O. Box 215, Grand Marais, MN 55604.

First printing 1982

Second printing 1986

ISBN 0-910259-04-6

Contents

First Cold	5
Rules for Winter	7
Bear Grazing	8
Gifts	9
Entering the Grand Portage Reserve	11
Powwow	13
Spring Comes to Grand Portage	15
Requiem for Clarence Fitch	17
Where I Bathe	18
Twelve Miles to the School Bus	19
Why I Live in These Hills	21

FIRST COLD

This first cold spell has cracked our lips and hands
And backed us to the fire nursing aches.
Eastward above the pines Orion starts
His climb, a lantern Jupiter before
Unshuttered on the snowy path. The place
We live has frozen 'round the shack but voices
Call: the river sounds of spirit women
Singing over icy rocks and shield.
The Manitou of winter here is up
And speaks tonight, and ancient in the north
The glowing sky flares tongues of cold-fire light.

RULES FOR WINTER

When it's time for sleepwalks to the cabin,
salute the stars and check the yeasty moon.
Listen for the owls. If you are lucky
there will be a row of holes
by morning where wolves walked.
Sleep cool in feathers.
Dream your lover moves to you through water.
Dress at dawn in cotton wool,
feed the children roses, buttered wheat,
raspberry tea. In autumn, only,
keep deer mice. When whiskey jacks
knock on the windows, wave
and watch them float. Set
fish for ermine in bird feeders
and expect squirrels to fly,
by night. Don't look
for heat from bleeding trees,
or sense from strangers rapping
at your door blind, deaf, and mainly dumb.
Serve laying hens fresh snow
and corn. Shovel wide,
for deep snow grow webbed feet,
and when the rain is freezing stay inside,
sniff sweetgrass rings, sing poems.

BEAR GRAZING

Across a yellow meadow
the black bear grazes,
bites lion's teeth,
spits bitter heads,
ripples slack and shiny pelt at flies,
licks ants.
Blind to us in the south,
it sniffs stiff wind
from north, hears
nothing of our joyful whispers,
feels ants, dandelions, flies,
not the waves of longing we send out
to sink our hairless hands into that shine
and lift to us the secret life of bears,
only guessed, shown now a gift
across a yellow meadow.

GIFTS

When I harvested last week
waist-deep in squash blossoms,
knees in beans, you wheeled in.
We joked of cabbage heads and slugs
while you took up from me
the vegetable life
your ruined liver bids,
clutching in your arms
the blood of beets, your hand
delicately wreathed
in a bouquet of parsley.

Friend, you first came to me
from painful harvest of a child,
her cousin drunken at the wheel,
grief clumsy under beer and jokes.
I had no garden then. You watched me
start to learn this stony place.
Then no bouquets,
but from your kill you gave,
ruffed grouse, moose meat,
once from the steaming gap
the bloody liver of a deer,
thrust warm into my hands.

ENTERING THE GRAND PORTAGE RESERVE

Between the shadow of the cut
Watch For Fallen Rock
and a royal isle at rest
the lake lies a leper
under peeling scabs of ice,
the blue lips briefly showing
beyond the bay when grey
lusterless skin shifts
and flakes again.
I am sailing in my steel
and snowtread-rubber craft
toward the scar across
the breast of Josephine
where fleets of trucks are slowed
to pull into her heart, as though
to hear an ancient beat of drums.
Mountain, island, lake
through which I navigate these days,
pale voyageur though I may be,
have marked a compass of dream
reserved to me and shall
go with me when I drift away.

POWWOW

The Drum of Bear Heart and the local Drum
applaud him to his feet, beat out of him
Anishinabe, shake the rusty old coat
off his ankles. Slowly, feeling every
socket in his bones, he sets the belt
around thin loins under his paunch, and moves,
unexpected, right into the circle.
All the dancing kids stand still. There are
no bells. The women by the door jamb
stop and lean, listen to the old man
joke his toothless challenges, and laugh.
Feathered boys cross smiles with him. No one
mocks his mix of words nor pities him.
He is who they are, their past, their future,
and Bear Heart Drum starts up the war dance he's been
asking for. Heavily he shuffles
once around the circle, pants pissed wet,
beer belly bloating out buttons of his ragged
shirt, pleased with himself and with the others,
in bright bustles, shawls, beads, moccasins,
who gravely move to join him, who keep
the rhythm he recalls them to, who dance.

SPRING COMES TO GRAND PORTAGE

In flapping, stained and wrinkled overcoats,
the two old ones, like two great ambling bears
roused from a fusty cave or hollow tree
by April's first warm invitation, lumber
down the hill from school to trading post.
Imperiously they flag me for a ride.
Their sexual energy, the April shine,
glows on their faces, flashes from their eyes,
grabs me on their beery breath like hugs.
They gather here for funeral rosaries,
today corpse-housing of the old Chief John,
and these survivors, Henry, Wilfred, feel
their youth, the life juice running maple sweet
in gnarled limbs. Tongues are thickly sugared
with sly compliments and lusts to make me
younger, nubile and naive, to draw,
by gaiety, bravado, courtly grace,
the circle 'round us in the morning light.
Sudden clouds of new-winged brown and yellow
butterflies cover the warm blacktop,
and snow lies rotting, loin-deep in the woods.

REQUIEM FOR CLARENCE FITCH

Old man in the boneyard,
long on the way to here
from the first pump of
lungs turned cracked
leather at the end, from
first clumsy steps
hung to brother's shirttail
through the dooryard mire, always
poverty snapping at your feet
in Depression dog days
across reluctant fields,
catting, logging, brushing a
living from forest fur, did you
know you were on the way to here?

In the last you took
eight days for two, not drugs
nor dragging breath
foreshortening, constricting,
hurrying you on, but the
inexorable moment. Black
watch cap, greasy overalls
and long johns gone,
bathed in a laying out
of cleanliness, stranger
without your smoky lineaments,
you stared with cradle eyes
and tugged the hospital shroud
to cover bony knees.

Who "wouldn't live nowhere
else" — and doesn't — did you know
the canker ate you eats us all?

Your dogs are singing
by your cabin door.
You are here at last, so rest.

WHERE I BATHE

Where I bathe
below rapids in clear water
cold over the stony floor
is crayfish country.
The gulls move downstream
to the bend and wait.
Darting from slippery rocks
the sudden crayfish bites,
small undertaker
tasting my mortality.

TWELVE MILES TO THE SCHOOL BUS

Travelers pass each other on
this potholed road like gods: at dawn
the white tailed deer verge, motionless,
a moose full-furnitured for mating
briefly bars the passage. Running
foxes harbinger for miles.

Phoebus in his Ford pickup,
the great disc blood red
burning at his back, his round
Anishinabe face sleepcreased
and watchful eyed, moves forth
on his appointed hunting path.
The west winds of his passing catch
the golden coins that strew the road
and get them quaking, quivering
alive, as when they were stem set.

Awesome, an autumnal kingdom
flares birch and aspen torches, springs
dry up this year, a white wolf flashes
on the road like light on tails
of mist that smoke across the marsh.
Portentous mornings follow each
on each to winter, shadows walk,
and in the evening great horned owls
call deeply, darkly from the hunt.

WHY I LIVE IN THESE HILLS

I stay here for the northern sky,
for stars caught in the hairy pines,
for moons that come at will and go
without a by-your-leave. No matter
if the evening rain clouds bank
the western gap up-river, or if
thunder groans over the mountains,
northward there will be the light.
I stay here for the sky outside
these windows, for the random shapes
of trees against a brightening
and paling glow, for smell and crackle
of a northern fire I can't set
or smother. Groggy as I make
my bed and check my clock, clumsy
with boot laces, buttons, yet
I come alive my lamp shut off,
and when at last I fall to sleep,
a northern pulse beats into mine.

Joanne Hart has lived on the Canadian Border 12 miles off Highway 61 since 1974. Her poems appear in many journals and in anthologies. A fine press chapbook, *The Village Schoolmaster,* was published in 1985 by The Bieler Press, Minneapolis.

Jayne Gagnon's art, mostly pen and ink and watercolor, has been exhibited throughout Minnesota. Her other interests include Indian arts and crafts and sled dog racing. She and her husband, Curtis, operate Portage Valley Store at Grand Portage.

Drawings:

Trout Lake from Mt. Sophie
Log Cabin on the Pigeon River
Hat Point and Grand Portage Bay
Powwow
Wilfred Montferrand and Henry Peterson
Pigskin's Cabin at Mineral Center
The Witch Tree

Reprints of drawings available from Jayne Gagnon, Grand Portage, MN 55605.